Sports Illustrated KIDS
HOCKEY Patterns

BY MARK WEAKLAND

CAPSTONE PRESS
a capstone imprint

Sports Illustrated Kids Rookie books are published by Capstone Press,
1710 Roe Crest Drive, North Mankato, Minnesota 56003
www.capstonepub.com

Library of Congress Cataloging-in-Publication Data
Cataloging-in-Publication data is on file with the Library of Congress.
ISBN 978-1-4765-0227-4 (library binding)

Editorial Credits
Anthony Wacholtz, editor; Ted Williams, designer; Eric Gohl, media researcher;
Eric Manske, production specialist

Photo Credits
Capstone Studio: Karon Dubke, 10–11, 22–23; Corbis: Icon SMI/Fred Kfoury, 16–17; Getty
Images: AFP/Cris Bouroncle, 28–29; Newscom: Getty Images/AFP/Cris Bouroncle, 26–27,
Icon SMI/Bob Frid, 6–7; NHLI via Getty Images: Steve Babineau, 12–13; Shutterstock:
Eric Fahrner, 8–9, Scott Prokop, 2–3; *Sports Illustrated*: Damian Strohmeyer, cover, David E.
Klutho, 1, 14–15, 18–19, 24–25, Robert Beck, 4–5, 20–21

Printed in the United States of America in North Mankato, Minnesota.
032013   007223CGF13

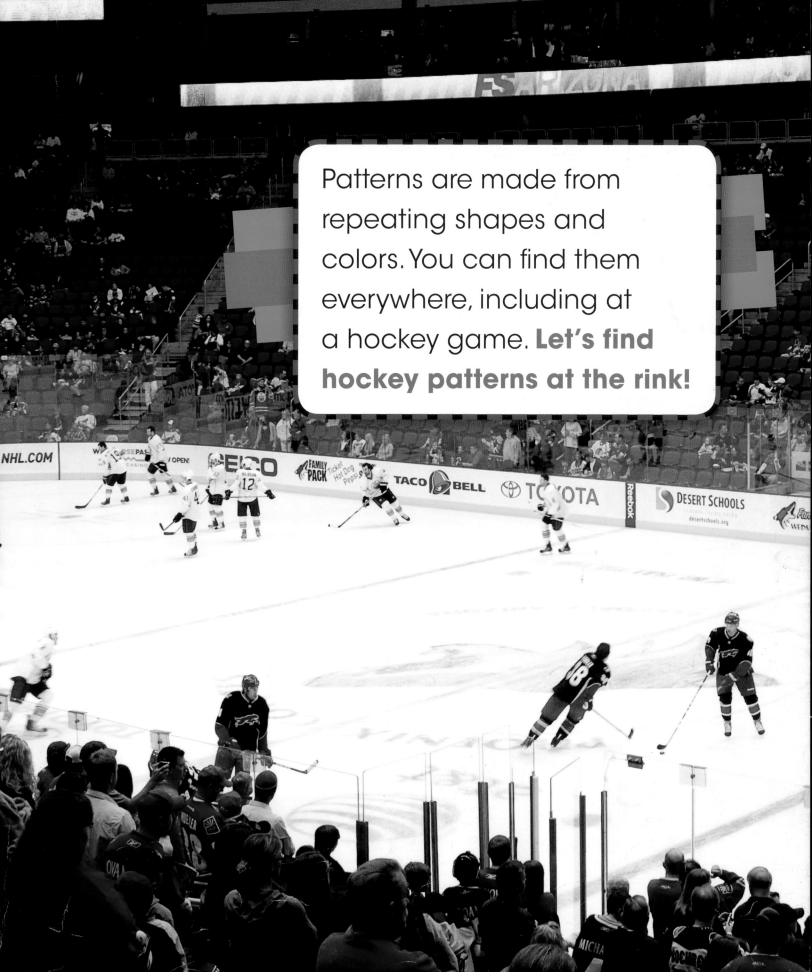

Patterns are made from repeating shapes and colors. You can find them everywhere, including at a hockey game. **Let's find hockey patterns at the rink!**

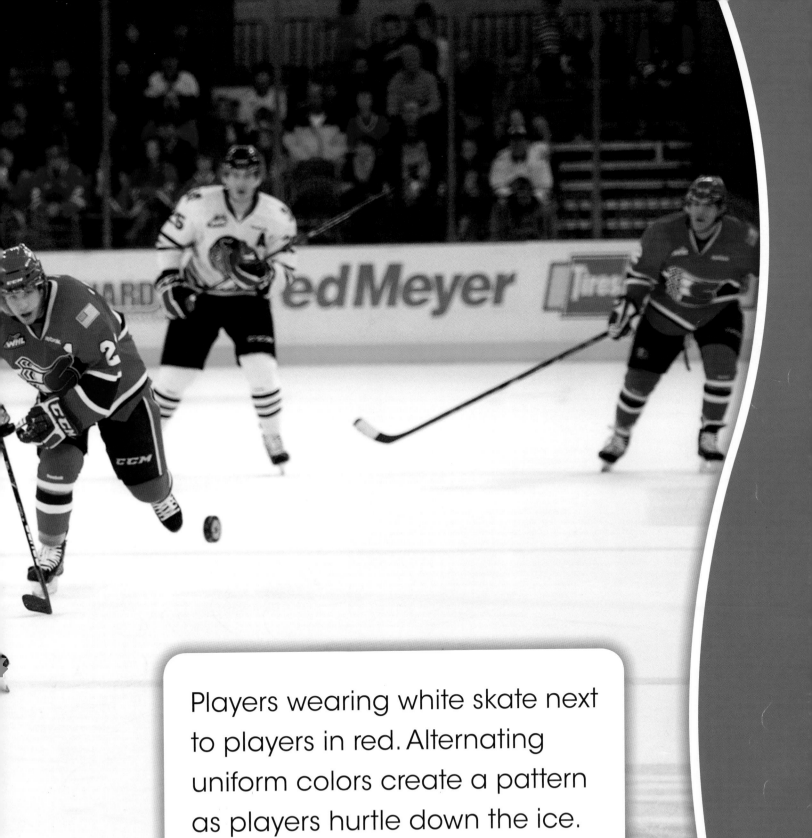

Players wearing white skate next to players in red. Alternating uniform colors create a pattern as players hurtle down the ice.

Fans turn a line of green and blue signs into a color pattern. What color would come next?

Referees wear a striped pattern. Even fast-moving players can easily see a referee's black and white stripes.

When lined up on a bench, hockey equipment makes a pattern. Do you see it? Each group of equipment has one helmet, one puck, and two skates.

Number patterns can be found in a triangle of pucks. Each row has one less puck than the row below it.

Players fight for the puck in front of a goal.
High above the action, patterns line the
roof of the arena. Look up and you will
see patterns of dark and light shapes.

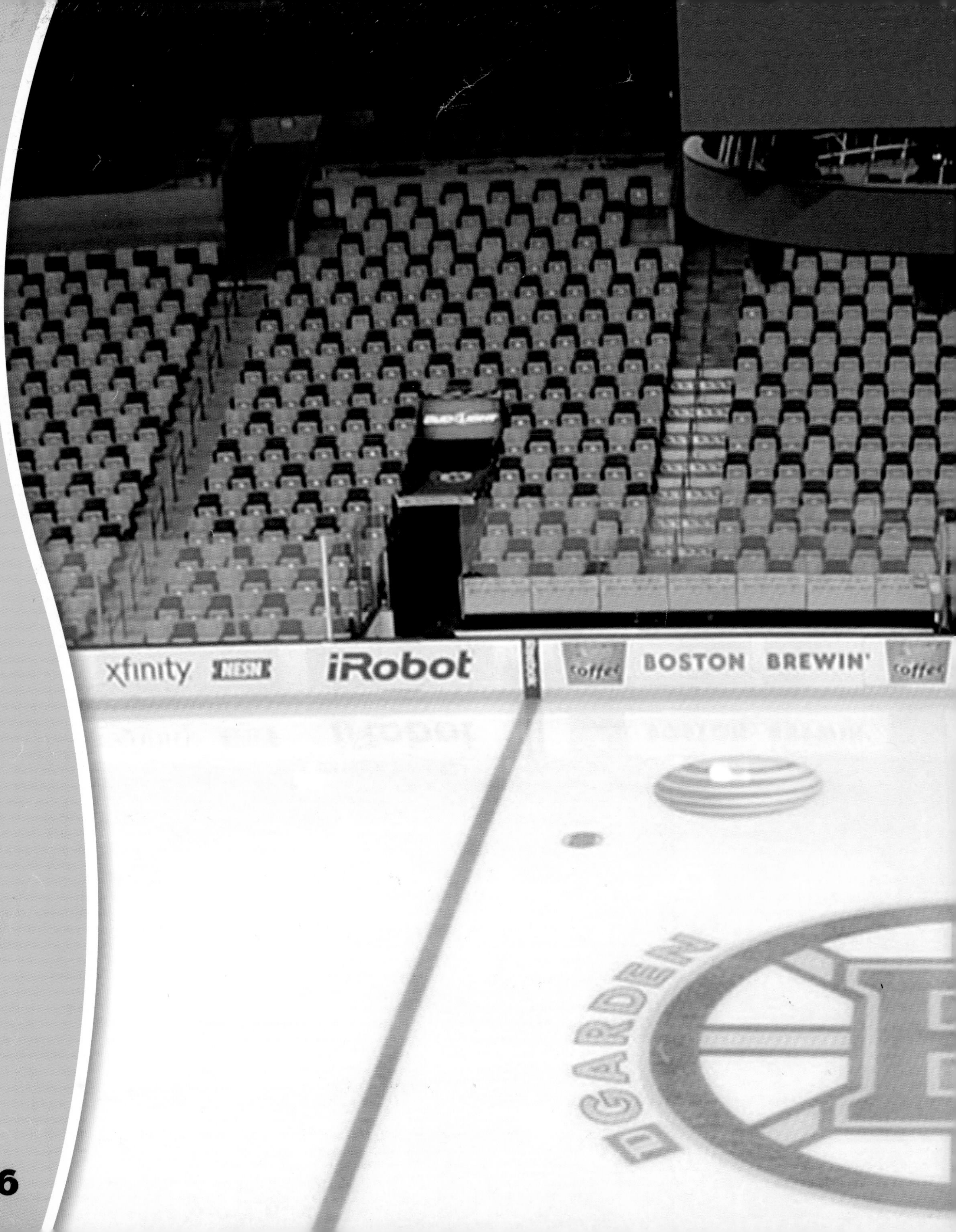
xfinity
NESN
iRobot
coffee
BOSTON BREWIN'
coffee
GARDEN

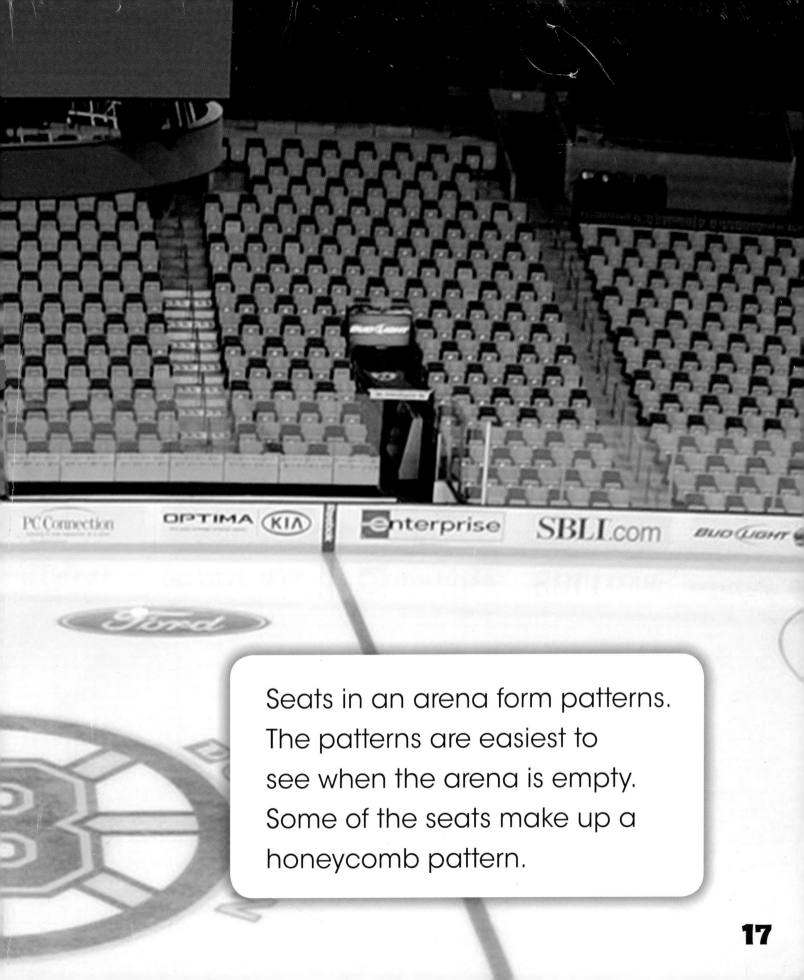

Seats in an arena form patterns. The patterns are easiest to see when the arena is empty. Some of the seats make up a honeycomb pattern.

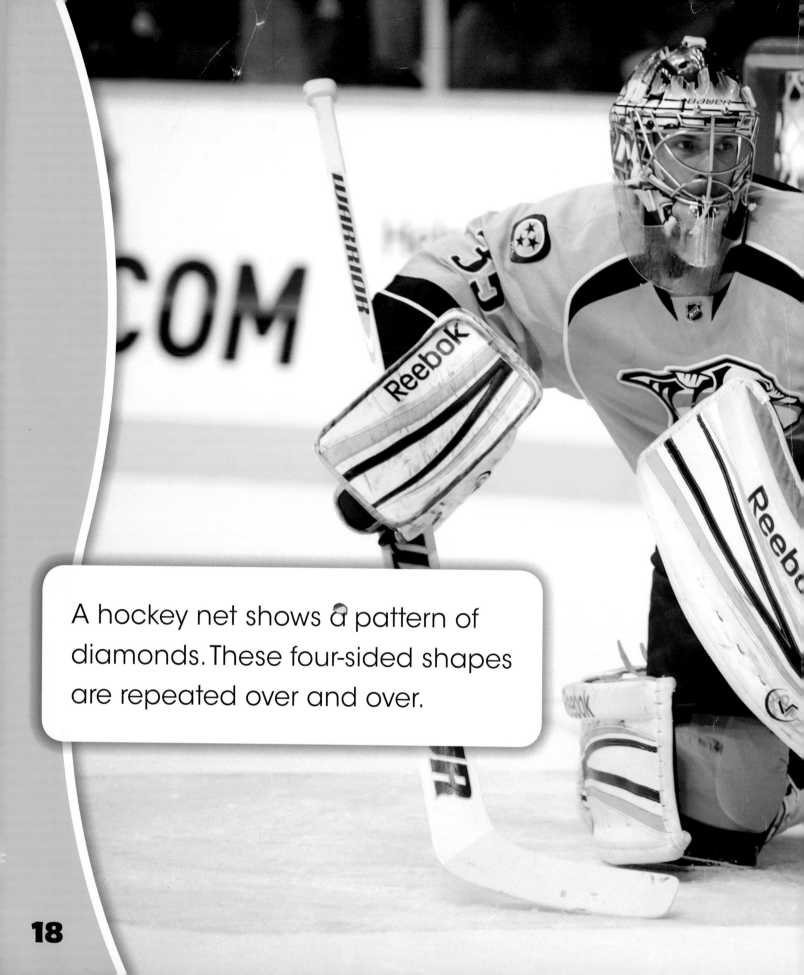

A hockey net shows a pattern of diamonds. These four-sided shapes are repeated over and over.

During a face-off, pairs of players dressed in blue and white make a pattern. But these players aren't looking for patterns. They're concentrating on the puck!

Resting blades and pucks make a number pattern on the ice. One blade, two pucks, one blade, two pucks. What comes next?

You can even find hockey patterns outside. Side-by-side hockey rinks create patterns of rectangles on a frozen lake.

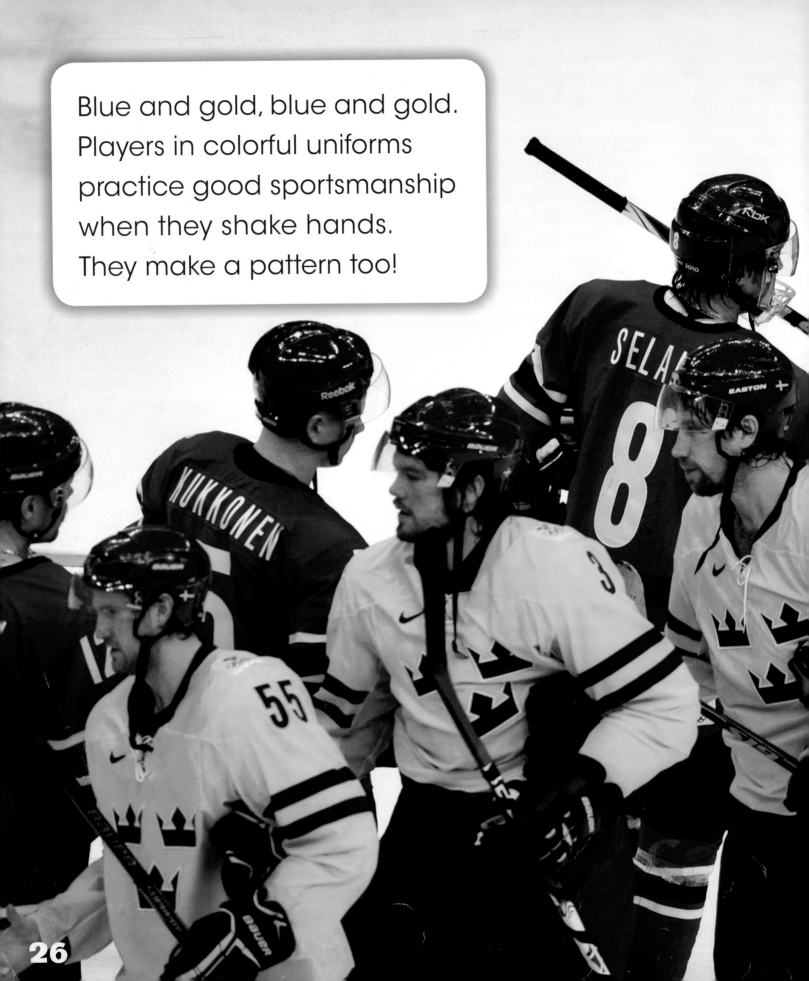

Blue and gold, blue and gold. Players in colorful uniforms practice good sportsmanship when they shake hands. They make a pattern too!

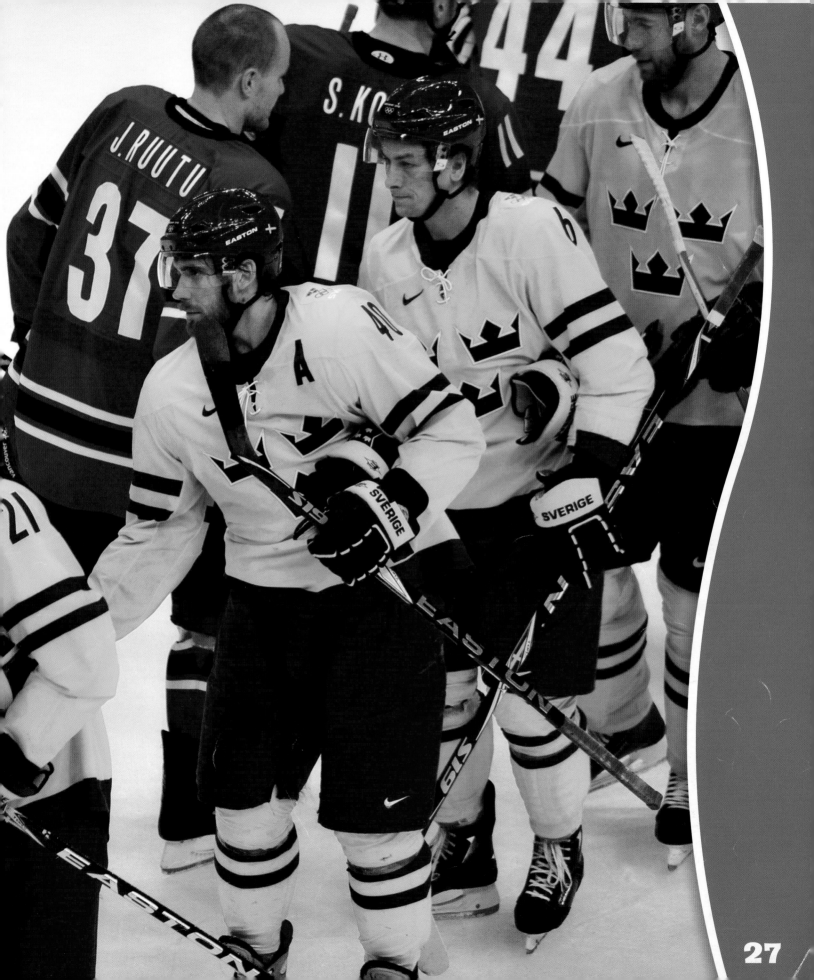

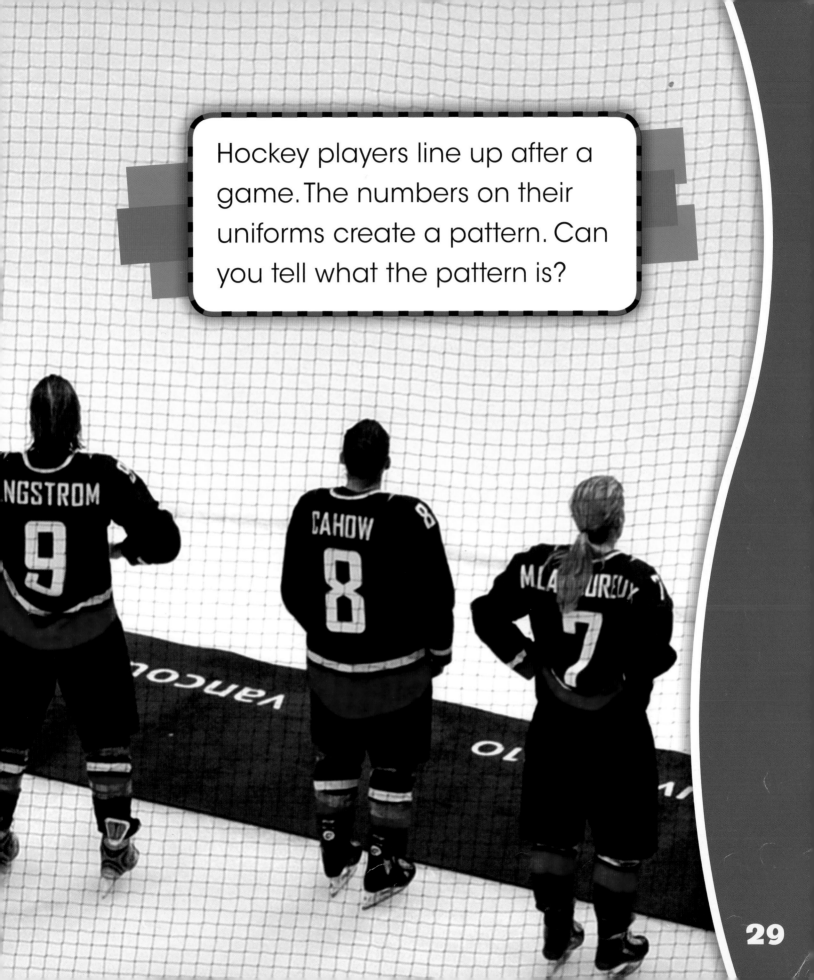

Hockey players line up after a game. The numbers on their uniforms create a pattern. Can you tell what the pattern is?

Glossary

alternating—going from one thing to another in a rhythm or pattern

arena—a large area that is used for sports or entertainment

diamond—a shape with four sides, like a square standing on one of its corners; a diamond is also called a rhombus

face-off—when a player from each team battles for possession of the puck to start or restart play

hurtle—to move quickly

referee—a person who supervises a sports match and makes sure that the players obey the rules

repeating—describes something that occurs over and over

sportsmanship—playing a sport or game respectfully and fairly; players shake hands as a sign of sportsmanship

Read More

Doeden, Matt. *Sidney Crosby: Hockey Superstar.* Sports Illustrated Kids. North Mankato, Minn.: Capstone Press, 2012.

Jordan, Christopher. *Hockey Opposites.* Plattsburgh, N.Y.: Fenn/Tundra, 2011.

Weakland, Mark. *Football Colors.* Sports Illustrated Kids. North Mankato, Minn.: Capstone Press, 2013.

Internet Sites

FactHound offers a safe, fun way to find Internet sites related to this book. All of the sites on FactHound have been researched by our staff.

Here's all you do:

Visit *www.facthound.com*

Type in this code: 9781476502274

Index